<u>Title:</u> The Seven Signs of Charisma

<u>Author & Illustrator:</u> Nick del Castillo

<u>Book Cover Information</u>: "The Mysterious Ferris Wheel" (oil on canvas) Nick del Castillo © 2010

<u>Books by Nick</u>:

"Virtues to Happiness" © 2016

"From Zero to Success!" © 2017

"Notions on Emotions" © 2020

<u>Dedication:</u>

This book is dedicated to Professor Wayne Finke.

Kindle Direct Publishing, 2nd Edition © 2024

Table of Contents:

1. <u>What is Charisma?</u>

What is charisma anyway? It is a social gift. This may be open to opinion, but charisma is that which exudes a gracious flair emanating from one's personality. Charisma is the gift that is associated with but not limited to attraction, social magnetism and the 'glow' that comes from the mere presence of a person. In other words, it is an attractive social grace that certain people seem to be endowed with. There are various qualities that a charismatic person may possess, but these do not necessarily add up to equaling 'charisma' and each charismatic person (like everyone else) is unique. Charisma is not good looks. Charisma is not leadership skills. Charisma is not a polished speaking voice. Charisma is not necessarily being extroverted. Charisma is not something one can learn, but if you have it, it can be developed and expressed. You know when it is there, but you cannot really put your finger on it as if you were pointing to an island on a map. Although some charismatic people may have a lot of friends and a large following, not everyone will agree that a particular individual is charismatic.

Why should I even care about charisma? Charismatic people, whether in influential positions or not, nevertheless possess powerful personalities. They can use their social charm for good or for bad purposes. The power of a charismatic person can attract people to a particular mission or they can seduce others via manipulation tactics. Some authors on charisma may argue that it is a skill that anyone can learn. Although it exists in various forms, degrees and has subjective elements, it is a gift in which you simply have it or you don't. You can learn good posture, how to make certain gestures or even learn how to tell jokes, but you will not necessarily become more charismatic per se.

Charismatic people are naturally attractive. It is almost as if their personality speaks for itself and communicates before the mouth has opened.

There is definitely an air of mystery, since charismatic people may not necessarily have outstanding attributes such as being rich, wise or popular, but when you meet one there is an uncanny attraction, a kind of 'social magnetism' that simply draws you in. It is analogous to the inexplicable quality found in relationships of what people call 'chemistry' or what can be referred to as 'clickability' (if such a word exists). Somehow people 'click' and seem to get along. They appear to be the right fit for one another like a hand to the glove. This is a bit puzzling since the person may not be the smartest, the richest, the prettiest, the most likeable etc... but somehow they match up and mutual harmony exists within the couple. Finding the right person is not about checking off a long list of qualities desired in a person, but about the person as a whole. It is also analogous to that of a sports team. It is not necessary for each player to be the best, in order to win a championship but it is essential that each teammate work together in order to win. A coach may want skilled players, but what is even more important is how the team meshes as a whole. The players may not be the fastest or the strongest, but together they succeed as one. It is the phenomenon of synergy in which $1 + 1$ can 'equal' 5. As the adage goes, 'the whole is worth more than the sum of its parts'. Thus, someone may not have all the desired qualities to have an attractive personality but somehow they are perceived as being charismatic. This is the crux of the mystery of charisma: What makes up charisma?

Charisma is being written about to share with you the greatness of this personality gift, but also to warn you of its potentially corruptive side in which people fall prey to. Charisma is not the most important gift in the world, but rather that of love. It is better to be a person of character and charity and than that of charm and charisma. There are patterns in every field of study. There are patterns in the charismatic personality that are about to be exposed. Some people may enjoy this book for entertainment purposes, some may have an 'aha!' moment and connect with the patterns and others may be able to understand the pitfalls and for some people, to be honest, may flat out disagree since they either do not understand the content, have a different experience or have defined the word 'charisma' in a different light…

2. <u>Difficulties in Defining Charisma</u>

Charisma is hard to define. It deserves to be under serious semantic scrutiny. In the field of linguistics, etymology will give you the origin of a particular word, but that original meaning may not correspond to its modern meaning and does not account for the context in which the word is used as well. No matter how well you describe something, language has its limits in explaining reality. This is especially true for immaterial concepts. Charisma is intangible, but it exists in tangible people. One may be energetic, spunky, sanguine, socially savvy, but not necessarily charismatic. 'Kharisma' is the Greek word for 'favor' or 'grace'. Charisma is a gift. Some may define charisma as a type of social charm that lures people in. Although this is true to some level, how that charm is manifested or where the attraction comes from is open to interpretation and can be quite enigmatic.

Even though charisma is not something that can be learned, some traits that a charismatic person displays can be learned to a certain extent. This depends on the person's innate abilities and their environment. Therefore, it is a blend of nature and nurture. Charisma is hard to classify, and it is also hard to isolate from other realities. The charismatic personality on a practical level can be generally defined, but it is hard to pin down on an intellectual level. It is difficult to separate charisma from other concepts and hard to know where one facet begins and where another ends. Although morality, beauty and intelligence are all separate topics of study, when they are lacking in a person, they can snuff out any charisma that they may have had in the first place. Charisma is hard to define since it is not completely independent of other qualities and there are overlapping areas that are open to debate. Another problem with defining charisma is in that of subjective feelings and perceptions. One person may be blown away by the charm and confidence of another person in which they are mesmerized by their perceived charismatic personality, but another person may not.

The problem with defining charisma is the absence in its ability to be tested. In other areas such as intelligence one can at least take an IQ test or measure intellectual abilities with memory tests and logical reasoning exams etc… but with charisma no such test exists, nor can exist. If you measure charisma with fame you may fall into the trap of a popularity contest or credit the person who has the best marketing techniques. Thus, this would be an error in pinning down the essence of charisma. There are measurements in the empirical world, such as in units like inches, kilometers, pounds, ounces etc. Let's face it, the physical world is measurable. Intelligence to one degree or another can be measured, but even then the data can be a bit fuzzy since there are different types of intelligence and different ways of measuring them. Every test has its flaws, but it is a lot harder to measure and to quantify charisma. Even though this may be the case, most people can detect that there are degrees of charisma. There are also ages in which a person may come off as more charismatic due to their looks and the spotlight that they are under, but when they are older, frail and with less energy they may not be perceived as having the same charisma as from before. Someone in a really bad mood can indeed be very charismatic, but it is temporarily suppressed because of their heated emotions.

Charisma is intimately tied with personality. Personality is yet another tricky concept to define which alone deserves its own deep study and extensive research. It is not important to have charisma, but it may be useful to know about it. Charisma can also be intermingled with musical or theatrical talent, but these are separate gifts. A person can be a great performer, but not necessarily charismatic and vice versa. Even in the realm of athletics, you can measure how much you can lift or how fast you can run, or how many points are scored in a game, but once again with charisma… Can it really be measured? Another problem in defining charisma is in the person or group defining the term. There are so many angles you can take in detecting charisma that some may overemphasize one area over another. If one notices charisma, does that imply that they themselves have it? Not necessarily, but charisma is relational. The social realm is inseparable from charisma and is part of its essence. A charismatic person will be able to catch on and in a sense be like a social chameleon and adapt to various social settings. It is paradoxical, but charismatic people tend to be both adaptable and natural at the same time. Charismatic people are social artists, and this is precisely where the social genius of the charismatic person comes into play. They are able to make smooth transitions without coming off as awkward or fake. Someone needs to have a certain level of social understanding to perceive charisma. Someone who is really smart can more easily detect intelligence in others since they themselves have it. Can a charismatic person more easily detect another charismatic person? Possibly since like attracts like. It would seem to be true that like knows like. Although not in all cases, it takes one to know one. The purpose of these pages is exposure to that which is open for an interesting discussion. Without further ado, here are the seven signs of charisma!

3. <u>Sign #1 - Open Body Language</u>

The charismatic person is constantly communicating. This ongoing communication is not always in words per se. The body is 'speaking' all the time. Dialogue occurs when there is openness. It is important to have openness, but not in forcing an opening. This openness can lead to a conversation and thus a better understanding of other people. Even though spoken words are significant, it is important to read another's body language in order to capture the person's mood. Moods can also be noticed from the tone of one's voice. Some people have the gift for reading people. Even though it may be the case, we all share and communicate how we feel with our physical bodies. In fact, our words speak mere blurbs, but our body speaks volumes of books! Before someone decides to start a conversation with a new person that they just met, the body is the first to 'speak'.

Someone who can pick up on body language, in a sense takes a metaphorical picture of that which is invisible in another person.

Charismatic people thrive on meeting new people due to their uncanny knack for openness to initiate a conversation. The first impression is the look that is portrayed, that is your body language. Before any word is spoken your body language starts 'speaking'. You can say that you are 'excited' in a monotonous voice while slouching in a chair and people will be able to catch on that your words do not match your body language and naturally will have a hard time believing you. When in doubt, we tend to consciously or subconsciously believe what we immediately see rather than what we may interpret on an intellectual level. If you move your hands up and say 'Wow! that roller coaster ride was a thriller!' You do not need to describe in detail how you feel since people can already feel your vibes. It is interesting to note just how much our body 'speaks'. Sometimes one's expressions can tell it all. Our minds pick up on things to inform us of something, but we are not exactly sure why we even got these thoughts in the first place. It could be that your mind saw an obscure pattern, had some form of deja vu etc....

Sometimes social savviness and charisma go hand in hand, but can a charismatic person be 'socially awkward'? Accurately defining social awkwardness is a challenge. No one is perfect and we all have our quirks and idiosyncrasies, but for lack of a better definition social awkwardness can be defined as objectively strange comments, gestures or actions which causes people to feel uncomfortable in a social setting. Given the apparent qualities of the quintessential charismatic person (if such a one exists), it would seem that social awkwardness and charisma are not only incompatible, but polar opposites.

Charisma as mentioned earlier is relational. Social relations involve one or more people. Relations are about connecting with others and we connect with others initially through our body language. So, if our body language is in a position that does not convey openness to dialogue, it can be hard to be or come off as charismatic. For example, if someone is looking at you straight in the face while conversing and you are staring down at their hands, this poor body language sends a signal to the person that they are not paying full attention and that their focus is elsewhere. A person who is socially awkward may not understand the unwritten rules of communication. For example, if someone says 'how are you?', most times people are not looking for a response of 'good' or 'bad' or even 'ok', but are actually trying to initiate a conversation about something which has more purpose or to get the person's attention. Sometimes they are trying to communicate but do not know how to do it. They seem to revert to clichéd politeness or apparently socially accepted phrases in which they are supposed to use in order to come off as socially normal, but since they do not fully understand the meaning behind these 'social textbook' tactics they come off as awkward. It is better to be silent and socially aware, than to speak in an attempt to appear 'normal'. There are different social customs in different countries and also things that people learn in order to be polite, but these are more in the areas of cultural customs and etiquette rather than social savviness. As with many fields, there are overlaps which once again, make intangible concepts harder to accurately define. Not everyone could be socially savvy, but everyone should try to be more understanding in general. Everyone has different gifts and charisma is not a final end. Knowing how to play the harp, or how to dodge in water polo are both skills, but they are not essential qualities. Nevertheless, every type of gift makes life a little more interesting for the world.

A charismatic person is not necessarily the person who talks up a storm and is constantly in the spotlight. They know how to soak in their environment and are constantly relating with their likeability via the art of listening. A charismatic person has a natural thermometer for noticing social energies. If someone's body language reads that they are jumping out of their seat to talk then the other person may yield and provide a nice outlet for the other person in need. On the other hand, if a person notices low energy, they might spice things up a bit by initiating a conversation. The language of the body is so powerful and full of meaning. Statistics time and again reveal that it communicates far more than the content of what you say. In summary, people tend to believe what they can easily pick via the senses and go with their 'gut instincts'. These gut instincts or uncanny intuitions are not based on charts and studies, but from what their subconscious mind picks up from the psychosomatic cues that they encounter via sense knowledge. Interpreting language and deciphering intellectual statements take time and training and do not come naturally to most people. A truly charismatic person is able to read body language and respond to it appropriately as well. They have the killer combo of being able to pick up on physical cues that have deeper meaning. They appear to be naturally genuine.

4. <u>Sign #2 - Genuine Naturalness</u>

Be natural, but do not try too much to be so. Being natural is tricky and not so simple. Here is the paradox: if you try too hard to be natural, you will come off as unnatural. So many things in life are about balance. If you eat too little, it is bad. If you eat too much it is bad. If you sleep too much it is bad. If you sleep too little it is bad. If you overthink things, it is bad, if you do not think at all, it is bad. Naturalness is itself a harmonious balance that breeds confidence and acceptance. Feigned energy or forcing charm will be immediately spotted as phony and you will quickly lose your credibility. Foreshadowing a future sign of charisma, confidence is attractive and people who are confident can lead with genuine naturalness. Naturalness is not doing exactly as you feel, but being yourself while keeping your manners and respecting others. Someone who is not endowed with natural charisma should not try to be so, but they should try to become a better person and the best version of themselves. Whether someone likes you or not is not your problem. It is their own issue to wrestle with. Be pleasing, but do not try to please the others. Being yourself is a great virtue, but not all charismatic people are virtuous. The naturalness of a charismatic person is not being uncouth or brash, but rather being the refined version of their natural selves. Being one's self is important especially in a social setting. Be comfortable in the environment that you bring and try to be socially aware.

5. <u>Sign #3 - Social Awareness</u>

Know the environment but do not overthink the situation. Acceptance of your situation and acceptance of your reality rather than preparing what you want to say. It is the focal point rather than the strategic preparation. Be like water. Water takes the shape of any and every container. Adapt to every social situation that you come across. It is not about planning per se. If you plan, you are done. 'Paralysis by over analysis' can happen to people who try to be attractive, but simply are not. The more they try, the more awkward they come off. It is like putting on the Chinese finger traps on your index fingers and pulling at the opposite ends with all your strength in order to remove them. Ironically, the harder you pull, the harder it is for your fingers to be set free. It is only when you relax and bring your fingers closer together that you are finally able to unlock your fingers from the traps. The device is purposefully counterintuitive. Some crafty salespeople will sometimes use the mirroring technique in which they try to imitate the person they are speaking with in order to connect with them. They do this by mirroring their accent or their speech patterns. Some charismatic people may use this technique to connect with people, but without appearing false. It is often a trait of the charismatic person to be able to connect with all different kinds of people. Charisma is never in isolation. The social component is totally essential in the charismatic expression. There is a mysterious interpersonal magnetism that goes on. A musician, a craftsman and an artist, can in a sense perform alone, yet the charismatic person feeds off of the people they are with.

A charismatic person is perceived as likeable due to social knowledge acquired from other people. If you really accept yourself and your environment you will never feel insecure. Insecurities arise from a lack of 'social ownership'. What this refers to is really saying what you mean and to mean what you say and to be ready to accept any backlash. Skipping ahead, that is why confidence is such a key social power. People who develop these social virtues will be more at ease and will therefore be able to potentially come off as more charismatic. Awkwardness is absent in the truly charismatic person and they are also able to diffuse awkwardness in a social setting. A charismatic person may be alone, but they are not necessarily lonely. They are comfortable with the presence of people, but also in their absence. This is the crux as to how a charismatic person differs from the quintessential extrovert. An extrovert gets energy from being around people and does not thrive in being alone. Whereas a charismatic person is adaptable. They tend to shine wherever they go yet, they also manifest poise and aplomb in most social environments.

Constant communication is good, especially in a relationship. In fact, many divorces happen due to a lack of communication. It is obvious that communication can be bad if it is fake. Falsehood does not provide any benefits to anyone. We cannot escape the world of communicating. It is inevitable. Even saying 'no comment' or not communicating at all in deadpan silence is in fact a form of communication. It is communicating that 'I don't want to talk'. Usually, charismatic people are expressive, and their expressions are a form of communication. It is in our human nature to want a return on your investment or in this example a social response. A charismatic person may also possess empathy but not all charismatic people will be moved to act on what they know and to accomplish good works. A person who notices the poor and marginalized may have a sensitive soul and do nothing for them, yet some charismatic people may notice the needs of the others and may help them out as well.

Empathy is a great quality, but also that of confidence.

6. <u>Sign #4 - Attractive Confidence</u>

It is in our human nature to seek out leadership. We tend to lean on role models and like to have someone to follow. People tend to gravitate toward confident leaders. Confidence is a very attractive personality trait. Most people lack confidence to one degree or another. Even the most confident people are not always confident. Someone who is likeable may attract a string of followers, but some people are able to draw them in simply with their 'attractive confidence'. Charismatic people are somehow able to display a natural confidence that people can detect. The person may or may not succeed in their venture and it may be for good or for bad purposes, but at the end of day they will be followed. The charismatic person is not necessarily the most intelligent person, but since they are socially confident from deep within, everything that follows seems to fall into place. This happens to be the case not because the sun is shining, because the money is available or because a specific plan looks like it will succeed, but because they are able to work with what they have. A salesperson might say: 'peanuts for sale! come buy some!' and someone replies, 'no thanks, I already have a bag' and then an unambitious salesperson replies 'ok, fine'. A person with confidence would reply: 'I know you have some, but what about an extra bag for your family' or 'do you know someone who does? I'm sure you do!' Once the mentality is set, the words, gestures and tone of voice follow along. If someone were to ask you 'do you have a blue car in the lot?' and do not know the answer, instead of losing a customer you may ask 'if I had a blue car in the lot, would you buy it?' This attractive confidence cannot be studied from a playbook as you would in football or even in the finding of a brilliant chess move. You really have to 'own it' and in a sense 'become it'. What is meant by 'own it' is to really, honestly say what you believe and believe what you say.

Words are very important and also very powerful, but the origin of our thoughts and feelings precede our words. First come our feelings and then our words follow. An infant is constantly communicating without even saying a single word, but they can 'say' quite a lot through their body language and tone of voice. People can develop confidence over time, but it is not something that you can learn from a textbook in school. It requires an act of the will. In other words it is something that you choose. People appreciate confidence, but not overconfidence where it becomes arrogance nor in the lack of confidence where it becomes pusillanimity. Perhaps Aristotle would agree with this since it falls within the golden mean (i.e. not too much and not too little). Confidence implies a risk since no one knows the future of an outcome. Just because someone is confident does not mean they will be successful. A charismatic person will naturally win people over via their attractive confidence. A person may be confident due to past successes, but what about the first success? They must somehow take the plunge from the strength within or it is possible that they have learned it from another person. Everyone is different, but there are patterns in people. Someone who is naturally charismatic may exhibit a portrayal of confidence, but this confidence is given from the people that the person is around. Someone that grows up with no one to help them to succeed will have a very difficult time being confident. Charismatic people are never born in a vacuum. We affect other people and other people affect us. There are few 'islands' out there. Most of us are closely connected to others' successes and failures. Many people lack confidence, but wherever there are a few that possess it, they bring with them a group of people. People often appreciate what they do not have, and see it in others.

Not everyone is cut out to be a professional athlete, yet

many spectators enjoy watching them play. Charisma can go

both ways: people who do not have it can appreciate it and

those that do, can understand what is going on and

appreciate a special personality in their midst. The

charismatic person may also display social creativity.

7. <u>Sign #5 - Social Creativity</u>

Resourcefulness not resources, the killer instinct not the ammo, it is knowing when to step in and when to kick back and to listen. It is about having social creativity and not the plastic smile. Creativity of approach but also being human. A charismatic person does not need to have all the answers in order to light up a room. In fact, they do not even have to know anyone's name per se. A charismatic person uses 'the night vision technique' in order to navigate in unknown social territories. Infrared night vision goggles are able to detect people or animals from the heat that they provide. A similar phenomenon happens on a social level. Just as with a little bit of heat people can be detected, the charismatic person is able to take a little bit of what they notice and run with it in order to make a social connection. When they lack info, they work around it in a natural and confident manner. A charismatic person may lack knowledge, but they will never lack the glow that they can share. The charismatic person is like a social Swiss army knife, they are able to use the right tool and utilize it with creativity. It is like golf. There are different sets of clubs depending on the situation at hand. Sometimes you need a putter for short range shots and at other times you need a sand wedge to get the ball out of the pit. Creativity comes from taking in what is out there and coming up with something new. In a philosophical sense nothing is strictly new or original since everything comes from something that is preexisting. Even original artists use priorly known elements to come up with something 'new'. Being creative is attractive as well as being creative with humor.

8. <u>Sign #6 - Well-Timed Humor</u>

The charismatic person will be spotted as having a sense of humor but at the right place and at the proper time. Someone who tries to be funny sometimes is not funny and is not necessarily charismatic. A charismatic person could be in a social setting in which it is not their intention to be in the spotlight and yet somehow that is precisely where they are placed. People could talk for hours and then at the right moment the charismatic person will chime in when their social intuition kicks in and will sometimes make people laugh, make people believe them, make people accept their charm and somehow make people feel attracted to them by the 'aura' that they emanate. It almost seems as if the charismatic person has a sixth sense of knowing how and when to chime in when other people are apparently in the spotlight. A charismatic person may not necessarily be an expert on human nature, but certain elements of knowing people are definitely at play. In knowing how people are and what they like, a charismatic person is able to come up with humor and to please the crowd. Everyone has their blind spots and cannot always be on top of their game. Sometimes people's humor can be tactless or misunderstood, but with social experience this can be mitigated. The best humor is that which comes from the heart. Most people know when other people are forcing something or trying too hard to be liked. Therefore, as the old adage goes, 'be yourself'. It is something only you can do. If you do so, you will have more charm.

9. Sign #7 - Magnetic Charm

A charming personality is able to move people's hearts. We are a blend of body and spirit. The visible affects the invisible and the invisible affects the visible. The 'art of the charm' that some charismatic people may have is quite disturbing since what the person proposes may make no logical sense, but they are somehow able to seduce the other person. We use logic, but we also have emotions. The charismatic person is able to send 'invisible signals' to hook the other person into accepting and believing in them. We all know what drugs and alcohol can do to alter one's state. Well, the same can be so with the 'radioactive waves' that the charismatic person emits sometimes just from the presence of the person. Sometimes people get so lured that they get trapped in relationship problems and fall for bad people. As the saying goes, they get lured 'hook, line and sinker'. It is only afterwards that they have suffered a great deal of manipulation that a person may say 'how could I have fallen for such a nasty and selfish person?' The answer is quite simple, the charm of the charismatic person drove the person so close to them 'like a moth to the flame' or together 'like peanut butter and jelly'. This charismatic charm can be analogous to electromagnetism. Two giant battle robots could be duking it out and one of them is able to control the other one with a powerful magnet. Suddenly, the controlled robot is subdued by an invisible force found in nature (i.e. magnetism). A similar thing happens with a charismatic person, on a social level. Beware of charismatic people, since they sometimes crave attention from almost anyone and everyone. Good looks can be deceiving, but charismatic charm can be a seductive poison dressed as a fancy perfume. For those who have fallen for such a person can sometimes look back and say: 'The person liked being liked, but they really didn't like me'. Those that have charm are aware of what attracts most people, they are aware that they have these qualities and then choose to exercise them. Being aware of this charm is not always easy to detect. Many people go with their gut feelings and the dictates of their emotions and do not stop to think if what they are charmed by is something beneficial or if it is detrimental. It almost seems as if sometimes subconsciously people like to be charmed, but definitely not fooled. Sometimes people are fooled by another's charm.

The tricky thing about charm is that not all personality types are attracted in the same manner. Some people may be more or less susceptible. The important thing is to know yourself. Whenever we feel charmed by a person, we need to take a step back from our emotions in order to discern what is going on. Once we realize the reality of what is happening then we should have the courage to fight off temptations and go for what is best. Not what feels good, but for what is good. For better or for worse, the charismatic personality type is prone to get the lion's share of attention from people. Oftentimes this attention is attained without having the person to even chase for it. People often flock to charismatic people and do not know exactly why. They will say this person is the most qualified or that is the best person to ask... but here is where the subconscious mind comes into play. On a subconscious level, people are superficially attracted to the charismatic person who is not necessarily the most qualified. Why is it the case that people pay thousands of dollars to motivational speakers who have limited education? People crave honest connections that a charismatic person can provide over titles and prestige. It is similar to the 'Dr. Fox Effect' in psychology. You have two professors, one is real and the other is fake. The fake professor is named 'Dr. Fox'. The real professor provides factual evidence, but is very boring and speaks in a monotone. On the other hand, Dr. Fox gives bogus answers but is an excellent presenter and full of energy. In the experiment, the students were then asked who the better professor was after having been taught by both and the majority of the people chose Dr. Fox. There is an unwritten language that charismatic people possess. Like knows like. Someone who is naturally charismatic will seemingly develop even more charisma due to 'social momentum' or what can be referred to as the 'snowball effect'. When a snowball starts rolling down the hill it starts gathering more snow making it bigger and bigger. So much so, that by the time the ball is at the bottom of the hill, it is now the size of a huge boulder. A charismatic person will receive more energy from people the more they get noticed and the more they learn from all the attention they receive. What is meant by the 'bright light effect' are external circumstances that feed a present reality. For example, someone may have a modest amount of charisma but if somehow that person has money, fame and power they may be perceived as being more charismatic than they really are due to the magnifying factors at play. Perception is not reality, but it sure has an impact on people's judgments and feelings. At the end of the day is charisma a benefit or a detriment?

10. <u>A Blessing or a Curse?</u>

Here is the dilemma. It is the tale of two realities in charisma. Is it a blessing or a curse? The charismatic person may be described as possessing the following attributes: a radioactive personality, buttery, relatable, energetic, socially savvy, charming, funny, socially creative, a connector, friendly, a social Swiss army knife, a human nature expert, socially tactful, adaptable, versatile, captures who you are and then runs with it, compliments without having people feel awkward, reads the social situation, knows what people want, captures all types of people, social assertiveness, attracts attention without drawing attention to themselves. Exhibit naturalness when alone, makes people feel comfortable, seeks connection without being needy etc… A charismatic person does not try too hard to get attention, but rather receives a lot of attention. Someone who is socially insecure may try to get attention and in doing so will fail since people can detect a needy person. Charismatic people know how to be likeable without seeking to be liked. When they are one on one, they are empathetic and make you feel special, when in a group they shine and add a special sparkle to their ambience. Charismatic people will make you feel as if you are the most important person in the room. Not all charismatic people have public speaking abilities, but the ones that do are able to do well since they often are good at connecting with their audience. People may be endowed with different gifts and talents, but unfortunately not everyone uses these towards their proper end, which is the good. Therefore, it is unfortunate that not every charismatic person is a noble one. Some general downsides of the charismatic personality are that they can be manipulative. They use their charm to attract people and then mislead them.

Some charismatic people come off as extremely likeable so people will buy into a bad idea from them such as going for a risky investment, in undertaking a dangerous voyage or in entering into a toxic relationship. Another common downside is that sometimes the charismatic person can be a bit fake. Since likeability is a trait that is often associated with the charismatic personality, sometimes the person can overdo it in wanting to be liked so they bend the truth about themselves or their environment in order to be liked even more so. Being liked is the 'drug' that some charismatic people binge on. Another foible they may possess is in 'guilt tripping' you. They use their social prowess to appear attractive and question you with their slick tongue to make it seem as if they are 'innocent' and that you are obviously 'guilty'. When other people perceive this to be true then you know their charisma has taken its effect in duping the others. Charismatic people can sometimes come off as people pleasers or 'yes men'. Although a truly virtuous person will call someone out when doing the right thing is what should be done, unfortunately sometimes charismatic people will choose ephemeral feelings over lasting truths. The worst potential downfall of the corrupt charismatic person is that of pride. Since charismatic people are so likeable or at the very least, often highly appreciated, they can fall into arrogance thinking that they are better than the others or look down on other people. A charismatic person needs to be aware of vanity. Popularity, fame etc. cannot be a substitute for self-esteem. It must come from within, or it will never be found from an unstable outside source. A charismatic person could fall into the trap of caring too much about what the others think of them. Having a beautiful personality is truly beautiful when it remains humble, otherwise it will be unbearably nasty. As the Latin phrase goes: 'the corruption of the best is the worst of all'. People who use their charisma for bad purposes see their gift as a selfish end in itself, but those that use it for the good, see it as a means for noble purposes.

We find ourselves when we get out of ourselves. We become who we are through other people. No one is successful alone. We communicate so that we can both understand and be understood. Whether people realize it or not we are constantly longing to be loved. Charismatic people need to be careful that the adulation they receive is not misunderstood as love or acceptance. That goes for any extraordinary person for that matter. People who are extremely rich or powerful have to be especially careful to decipher who are their real friends, who are the phonies and who are the foes. Even though charisma can play an important role and is a special gift, at the end of the day it is not that important. What really matters is charity and being a virtuous person. Charisma in a sense is not good or bad. It is a phenomenal grace that can be used to attract, lead and inspire many people. At the end of day, doing good works, performing your job well, being patient and striving to be a better human being is what really matters. Do you have all seven signs of charisma? Just a few? or do you disagree on what makes a charismatic person? Anyway, if you think you have charisma use it for the good so that the others may shine. If you do not have charisma, it really does not matter. Being happy and cheerful are far more important than having charisma.

11. <u>Epilogue</u>: from "Virtues to Happiness"

"27. <u>Cheerfulness</u>

Although life may come with hardships, we could always live the virtue of cheerfulness. Cheerfulness does not mean someone that always smiles or laughs, but someone whose happiness is based on virtue and knowing that they are loved. Some people may appear to be cheerful based on their personality or their natural disposition, but in some cases it is just a façade. Each person is truly a mystery and ultimately no one really knows the true state of a person's mind or even their intentions. Although it may be difficult or even impossible to really know another's true state of mind, we know our own state and can always strive toward greater perfection in the virtue of cheerfulness. If we want to make the world a greater place, we have to begin by first changing ourselves. We need to help people who are frowning on the inside to smile, and for those who are smiling to share it with others. We cannot give what we do not have. People are often cautious of sharing material goods, due to its scarcity in the dimensions of time and space. On the other hand, the immaterial goods of virtue and goodness are multiplied when they are shared and transcend the realms of both time and space. No one can change your attitude except you. So begin today, if you are not happy, try to make somebody else happy and I can assure you that you will have been successful in being happier.

Some ways to live the virtue of cheerfulness:

1) Think more of how you can serve the others rather than yourself.

2) Work hard and focus. If you do, less likely for your mind to wander on stupidities that may cause you to be unhappy.

3) Love? Yet again the cure all... Yes. As Virgil states:

"Omnia vincit amor." 'Love conquers all'. If you have true love [for the] others you may be hurt for putting your heart in [the] front lines, but you will be cheerful in the long run."

(from "Virtues to Happiness © 2016")

www.ingramcontent.com/pod-product-compliance
Lightning Source LLC
Chambersburg PA
CBHW071240240726
48654CB00009B/1140